The Browni
Ki

Written by Julia Donaldson
Illustrated by John Eastwood

Heinemann

Joy and Roy had garden trowels
For digging in the ground.
'Look, Roy!' said Joy. 'Come over here
And see what I've just found!'

A teapot, old and round and brown!
It had a broken spout.
Just then they heard a tiny voice.
It shouted, 'Let me out!'

The tiny voice grew louder.
Joy put the teapot down.
She lifted off the lid and saw
A little boy in brown.

His hair was brown. His eyes were brown.
He had a pointed nose.
And from his baggy trousers
Stuck out his pointed toes.

He had white powder on his face,
All floury, like a clown.
He had a flower in his hand.
He wore a tiny crown.

'I thank you,' said the boy in brown,
And gave a little bow.
'I am the Brownie King,' he said.
'I want to help you now.
This flower of mine is magic.
It has the power, you see,
To change you into animals.
What do you want to be?'

‘I want to be a mouse!’ said Joy.
‘Make Roy a mouse as well.’
The Brownie waved his magic flower
And said a magic spell.

Then Roy and Joy were round brown mice.
They pattered all around.
'I am enjoying this,' said Joy,
But Roy looked up and frowned.

A big brown owl was swooping down.
It had an open beak.
'An owl!' Roy howled, and Joy let out
A tiny little squeak.

'Help us, Brownie, help!' squeaked Joy.
'Please use your magic power.'
'Yes! Change us into cows!' said Roy.
The Brownie waved his flower.

Then Roy and Joy turned into cows.
Roy ate the grass and mooed.
'Stop mooing with your mouth full, Roy,'
Said Joy. 'It's very rude.'

Just then a cowboy came along
and Joy joined in Roy's moo.
The cowboy had a coil of rope.
Joy mooed, 'That's his lasso!'

The cowboy galloped down the hill
And waved his rope about.
'He's rounding up the cows!' said Joy.
'Quick, Brownie, help us out!
Please use your magic power again.
We've got no time to lose.
Please wave your flower and change us
Into baby kangaroos.'

Now Joy and Roy were in a pouch.
They had a bouncy ride.
'I am enjoying this!' said Roy.
'Yes, this is fun!' Joy cried.

But soon the ground got very hard
And Roy said 'Ow!' and 'Ouch!
I want to be a boy again.
It's bumpy in this pouch.'

'I want to be a girl!' said Joy.
The Brownie waved his flower,
And Roy and Joy were home again.
Their mum said, 'Have a shower!'

When Joy and Roy got off to sleep
They dreamed about lassoes,
And mice and owls and magic flowers
And cows and kangaroos.